Girls with Autism:
"Overcoming Diagnostic Challenges".

Julie White

Copyright

Table of contents

<u>Conclusion</u>

Introduction

Girls with Autism: Overcoming diagnostic challenges is a topic that addresses the unique difficulties and barriers that exist when it comes to identifying and diagnosing autism spectrum disorder (ASD) in girls. There are a number of factors that contribute to this diagnostic challenge, including a lack of understanding of the ways in which autism presents differently in girls, as well as a lack of awareness and recognition of the signs and symptoms of autism in girls.

Autism Spectrum Disorder (ASD) is a neurodevelopmental disorder that affects social interaction, communication, and behavior. The diagnosis of autism in girls can be challenging because the symptoms of autism in girls may be different from those in boys, and girls are often better at masking or hiding their symptoms.

Some research suggests that girls with autism may have more subtle symptoms, such as difficulties with social interaction, communication, and emotional regulation, rather than the more obvious symptoms often seen in boys, such as repetitive behaviors and limited interests. Girls with autism may also be more likely to have co-occurring conditions, such as anxiety or depression.

Additionally, diagnostic tools and criteria for autism were developed based on research primarily on boys, which can lead to underdiagnosis of autism in girls.

It is important to be aware of the potential diagnostic challenges in girls with autism and to use a multidisciplinary approach in the assessment process, including input from psychologists, psychiatrists, speech therapists, and other professionals.

Therapies and interventions that target the specific needs of girls with autism, such as social skills training, cognitive-behavioral therapy, and parent-mediated interventions, may be helpful in addressing the challenges they face.

One of the main reasons that girls are often underdiagnosed with autism is that the diagnostic criteria for autism were developed based on research and studies that primarily included boys. This has led to a bias in the diagnostic process, with girls being more likely to be overlooked or misdiagnosed with other conditions. Additionally, girls with autism may be more likely to mask their symptoms or conform to societal expectations, which can make it more difficult to identify the signs of autism in them.

Another factor that contributes to the diagnostic challenge for girls with autism is the lack of awareness and recognition of the signs and symptoms of autism in girls. Many people have a preconceived notion of what autism looks like, and this often involves stereotypical characteristics such as difficulty with social interactions, lack of interest in socializing, and repetitive behaviors. However, these characteristics may be less obvious or present differently in girls with autism, making them more difficult to identify.

There are also some unique challenges that girls with autism face that may contribute to the diagnostic challenge. For example, girls with autism may be more likely to experience anxiety and depression, which can be mistaken for symptoms of other conditions. Additionally, girls with autism may be more likely to experience difficulties with communication and social interactions, which can make it more difficult for them to express their needs and wants and make it harder for others to understand them.

In order to overcome these diagnostic challenges and ensure that girls with autism receive the support and services they need, it is important to raise awareness and understanding of the ways in which autism presents differently in girls. This can be done by increasing research on autism in girls, training healthcare professionals and educators to recognize the signs and symptoms of autism in girls, and working to create more inclusive and understanding environments for girls with autism.

Overall, Girls with Autism: Overcoming diagnostic challenges is a complex and multifaceted topic that requires a deeper understanding of the unique challenges that girls with autism face and the ways in which autism presents differently in girls. By raising awareness, understanding, and addressing the barriers to diagnosis, we can work to ensure that girls with autism receive the support and services they need to thrive.

Information on the diagnostic challenges faced by girls with autism, including why they may be underdiagnosed or misdiagnosed.

Autism is a complex developmental disorder that affects communication, socialization, and behavior. While it affects both males and females, there is growing evidence to suggest that girls with autism may face unique diagnostic challenges. This is because the symptoms of autism in girls may present differently than in boys, and as a result, girls are more likely to be underdiagnosed or misdiagnosed.

One of the biggest diagnostic challenges for girls with autism is the common misconception that autism is a "male disorder." This stereotype is based on the fact that autism is four to five times more prevalent in boys than in girls.

The misconception that autism is a "male disorder" can have a significant impact on the identification and treatment of girls and women with autism. Because autism is often thought of as a disorder that primarily affects boys, girls and women may be less likely to be diagnosed with the condition.

Additionally, girls and women with autism may be more likely to have their symptoms overlooked or dismissed as being "less severe" than those of boys. This can lead to a lack of appropriate support and services for girls and women with autism, and can also contribute to feelings of isolation and lack of understanding.

Furthermore, the stereotype of autism being a "male disorder" can also lead to girls and women being underrepresented in research studies, which can result in a lack of understanding about the unique experiences and needs of female individuals with autism.

In general, the misconception that autism is a "male disorder" can lead to girls and women with autism not getting the support and services they need to succeed in life, and can also perpetuate misunderstandings about autism and the experiences of those who live with it.

As a result, many healthcare professionals and educators may not be as attuned to the signs of autism in girls, leading to delayed or missed diagnoses. Additionally, girls with autism may be more likely to mask their symptoms, or to present with fewer or more subtle symptoms than boys, which can further complicate the diagnostic process.

Another diagnostic challenge for girls with autism is that the current diagnostic criteria for autism may not fully capture the experiences of girls. This is because the criteria were developed primarily based on research and observations of boys with autism.

The current diagnostic criteria for autism, as outlined in the Diagnostics and Statistical Manual of Mental Disorders (DSM-5) and the International Classification of Diseases (ICD-11), may not fully capture the experiences of girls with autism. This is because the criteria were developed based on observations and research of primarily boys and men with autism, and may not accurately reflect the ways in which autism presents in girls.

For example, many girls with autism may have more subtle or atypical symptoms than boys, such as difficulties with social communication that are not as severe or consistent as those typically seen in boys with autism. Additionally, girls with autism may be better able to camouflage their symptoms, or may be more likely to engage in social behavior that is considered "typical" in order to fit in with their peers.

Furthermore, research suggests that girls with autism may be more likely to have co-occurring conditions, such as anxiety and depression, which can further complicate their diagnosis.

Therefore, the current diagnostic criteria may not be sensitive enough to capture the unique experiences of girls with autism, and may lead to girls and women being underdiagnosed and undertreated. This highlights the need for more research on autism in girls and women, as well as the development of more gender-specific diagnostic criteria that take into account the unique ways in which autism can present in girls.

As a result, girls with autism may not meet all of the criteria for diagnosis, leading to missed or incorrect diagnoses. Furthermore, girls with autism may present with different symptoms than boys, such as social anxiety, depression, or eating disorders, which can lead to misdiagnosis of other conditions.

The underdiagnosis and misdiagnosis of autism in girls can have serious consequences, as it can delay access to appropriate services and support.

The underdiagnosis and misdiagnosis of autism in girls is a well-documented issue in the field of autism research and clinical practice. Several factors contribute to this problem, including:

Bias in diagnostic criteria: As mentioned earlier, the current diagnostic criteria for autism were developed based on observations and research of primarily boys and men with autism, and may not accurately reflect the ways in which autism presents in girls. This can lead to girls and women with autism being overlooked or misdiagnosed with other conditions.

Social expectations of girls: Girls are often expected to be more socially skilled and emotionally expressive than boys. Girls with autism may be able to camouflage their symptoms better, or may be more likely to engage in social behavior that is considered "typical" in order to fit in with their peers. This can make it more difficult for clinicians to identify autism in girls.

Different referral patterns: Boys are more likely to be referred for autism evaluations than girls, which can contribute to girls being underdiagnosed.

All these factors combined can lead to girls with autism being overlooked or misdiagnosed, which can have significant negative impacts on their mental health, educational and social development, and overall quality of life.

As a result, there is a need for greater awareness of the unique ways in which autism can present in girls, as well as the development of more gender-specific diagnostic criteria and training for healthcare professionals on how to better identify and diagnose autism in girls.

Girls with autism may not receive the specialized education and therapy they need to reach their full potential. Furthermore, girls with autism may be more likely to experience bullying, isolation, and other negative social outcomes as a result of their undiagnosed or misdiagnosed condition.

To address the diagnostic challenges faced by girls with autism, it is important to raise awareness of the unique symptoms and characteristics of autism in girls, and to train healthcare professionals and educators to recognize these signs.

Autism in girls can present with a wide range of symptoms and characteristics, many of which may be different from those seen in boys with autism. Some of the unique symptoms and characteristics of autism in girls include:

Social communication difficulties: Girls with autism may have more subtle or atypical social communication difficulties than boys. They may have difficulty initiating and maintaining social interactions, understanding social cues, or reading nonverbal communication.

Repetitive behaviors and interests: Girls with autism may have similar repetitive behaviors and interests as boys, but they may be less pronounced or more socially appropriate. For example, a girl with autism may have a strong interest in a specific topic, but may be more likely to talk about it with others and to make friends who share the same interest.

Emotional regulation: Girls with autism may have difficulty regulating their emotions, which can lead to mood swings, anxiety, and depression.

Masking: Girls with autism may be better able to camouflage their symptoms, or may be more likely to engage in social behavior that is considered "typical" in order to fit in with their peers. This can make it more difficult for clinicians to identify autism in girls.

Co-occurring conditions: Girls with autism are more likely to have co-occurring conditions such as anxiety and depression, which can further complicate their diagnosis.

It's important to note that these are general tendencies and not all girls with autism will have all these symptoms. Every individual with autism is unique and their symptoms and characteristics can vary widely.

Additionally, research on autism in girls needs to be expanded to better understand the unique experiences of girls with autism and to develop more appropriate diagnostic criteria. Furthermore, parents and caregivers of girls with autism can play an important role in advocating for appropriate services and support, and in providing girls with autism with the tools they need to overcome the diagnostic challenges.

In conclusion, girls with autism face unique diagnostic challenges, which can lead to underdiagnosis and misdiagnosis. This can have serious consequences for their access to appropriate services and support, and can negatively impact their development and well-being. It's important to raise awareness of the unique symptoms and characteristics of autism in girls, to train healthcare professionals and educators to recognize these signs, and to expand research on autism in girls to better understand their experiences and develop more appropriate diagnostic criteria.

Strategies and resources for overcoming these diagnostic challenges and getting the appropriate support and services.

Overcoming the diagnostic challenges faced by girls with autism is essential for ensuring that they receive the appropriate support and services they need to reach their full potential. There are a variety of strategies and resources available to help with this process, which can be used by parents, caregivers, healthcare professionals, and educators.

One key strategy for overcoming diagnostic challenges is early identification and early intervention. Early identification of autism in girls can improve their outcomes and increase the chances that they will receive the appropriate support and services. This can involve regular developmental screenings and evaluations, as well as education and training for healthcare professionals and educators to recognize the signs of autism in girls.

Early identification of autism in girls can help overcome many of the diagnostic challenges faced by this population. Some of the ways early identification can help include:

Facilitating earlier access to interventions: Early identification of autism allows for earlier access to interventions such as occupational therapy, speech therapy, and behavioral therapy. These interventions can help improve social communication, reduce repetitive behaviors, and promote overall development in girls with autism.

Improving educational outcomes: Early identification of autism can also lead to earlier interventions in the educational setting, which can improve educational outcomes for girls with autism. This can include providing specialized instruction and accommodations in the classroom, as well as working with educators to understand and support the unique needs of girls with autism.

Reducing mental health issues: Early identification of autism can also lead to earlier interventions to address co-occurring mental health conditions such as anxiety and depression, which are more prevalent in girls with autism. This can improve the overall quality of life for girls with autism.

Addressing the social challenges: Early identification of autism can also help address the social challenges that girls with autism often face, such as difficulty making friends, understanding social cues, and navigating social interactions.

Tailored interventions: Early identification can also help to provide more tailored interventions that take into account the unique ways in which autism can present in girls.

Overall, early identification of autism in girls can lead to better outcomes and improved quality of life for this population.

Additionally, early intervention programs, such as Applied Behavior Analysis (ABA) therapy, can help girls with autism to develop the skills they need to succeed in school and in social situations.

Early intervention can help overcome many of the diagnostic challenges faced by girls with autism by providing targeted support and services that address the unique needs of this population. Some of the ways early intervention can help include:

<u>Improving social communication</u>: Early intervention can help improve social communication skills in girls with autism, which can be more subtle or atypical than in boys. This can include interventions such as speech therapy, social skills training, and specialized instruction in the classroom.

Reducing repetitive behaviors: Early intervention can also help reduce repetitive behaviors and interests in girls with autism, which can be less pronounced or more socially appropriate than in boys. This can include interventions such as occupational therapy, behavior therapy, and specialized instruction in the classroom.

Addressing emotional regulation: Early intervention can also help address difficulties with emotional regulation in girls with autism, which can lead to mood swings, anxiety, and depression. This can include interventions such as cognitive-behavioral therapy, occupational therapy, and specialized instruction in the classroom.

Improving educational outcomes: Early intervention can also lead to earlier interventions in the educational setting, which can improve educational outcomes for girls with autism. This can include providing specialized instruction and accommodations in the classroom, as well as working with educators to understand and support the unique needs of girls with autism.

Addressing the social challenges: Early intervention can also help address the social challenges that girls with autism often face, such as difficulty making friends, understanding social cues, and navigating social interactions.

Overall, early intervention can help to improve the overall outcomes and quality of life for girls with autism by addressing the unique diagnostic challenges faced by this population.

Another important strategy is to advocate for appropriate services and support. This can involve working with healthcare professionals and educators to ensure that girls with autism receive the appropriate diagnosis and access to specialized education and therapy.

Additionally, it can involve working with government agencies and insurance providers to ensure that girls with autism receive the financial and medical support they need. Parents and caregivers can also seek out support groups, organizations, and online resources to connect with other families and individuals affected by autism and to gain access to information and resources.

It's important for parents and caregivers to be informed about the latest research and developments in the field of autism, particularly as it relates to girls. This can help them to understand the unique experiences of girls with autism and to make informed decisions about diagnosis, treatment, and support. Furthermore, it can help them to stay up-to-date on the latest therapies, interventions, and other services that may be beneficial for their daughters.

Advocating for appropriate services and support can help overcome many of the diagnostic challenges faced by girls with autism by ensuring that they receive the care and resources they need to succeed. Some of the ways advocating for appropriate services and support can help include:

Ensuring access to appropriate interventions: Advocating for appropriate services and support can help ensure that girls with autism have access to interventions such as occupational therapy, speech therapy, and behavioral therapy, which can help improve social communication, reduce repetitive behaviors, and promote overall development.

Improving educational outcomes: Advocacy can also help improve educational outcomes for girls with autism by ensuring that they have access to appropriate accommodations and specialized instruction in the classroom, as well as ensuring that educators have the training and resources they need to support girls with autism.

Reducing mental health issues: Advocacy can also help to reduce mental health issues such as anxiety and depression in girls with autism by ensuring that they have access to appropriate mental health services and support.

<u>*Addressing the social challenges*</u>: Advocacy can also help to address the social challenges that girls with autism often face, such as difficulty making friends, understanding social cues, and navigating social interactions, by ensuring that they have access to appropriate social skills training and support.

<u>*Raising awareness*</u>: Advocating for appropriate services and support can also raise awareness about the unique needs of girls with autism and the importance of addressing the diagnostic challenges faced by this population.

Overall, advocating for appropriate services and support can help to improve the overall outcomes and quality of life for girls with autism by ensuring that they receive the care and resources they need to succeed.

Another key strategy is to provide girls with autism with the tools they need to overcome the diagnostic challenges. This can involve providing them with social skills training, communication training, and other therapeutic interventions that can help them to develop the skills they need to succeed in school and in social situations.

Additionally, it can involve providing girls with autism with the tools they need to advocate for themselves, such as self-advocacy training, and teaching them how to communicate effectively with healthcare professionals and educators.

Providing girls with autism with the appropriate tools and support can help to overcome diagnostic challenges by increasing the likelihood that they will be accurately diagnosed and receive appropriate treatment and accommodations.

This can lead to improvements in their quality of life, including in areas such as communication, social interaction, and independence. Additionally, providing girls with autism with the tools they need can also help to reduce the negative effects of undiagnosed autism, such as anxiety and depression.

Some tools that may be helpful for girls with autism to overcome diagnostic challenges include:

Access to specialized assessments: Girls with autism may present differently than boys with autism, and specialized assessments that take this into account can help to ensure an accurate diagnosis.

Education and awareness for healthcare providers: Providers should be educated about the unique ways that autism can present in girls and how to recognize and diagnose it.

Support from a multidisciplinary team: Girls with autism may benefit from a team that includes professionals from different fields, such as psychology, psychiatry, speech therapy, and occupational therapy.

Access to appropriate treatment and accommodations: Once diagnosed, girls with autism may benefit from evidence-based interventions and accommodations that are tailored to their individual needs and strengths.

Support groups and mentorship: Connecting with other girls and women on the autism spectrum can provide a sense of community and validation, and mentorship can help girls with autism navigate the unique challenges they may face in their daily lives.

Positive representation of girls with autism in media and society: Positive representation of girls with autism in media and society can help to reduce the negative stereotypes and misconceptions around autism that can make it harder for girls to get diagnosed and accepted in the society.

In conclusion, overcoming the diagnostic challenges faced by girls with autism is essential for ensuring that they receive the appropriate support and services. Strategies and resources available include early identification and intervention, advocacy for appropriate services and support, staying informed about the latest research and developments in the field of autism, and providing girls with autism with the tools they need to overcome the diagnostic challenges. These strategies can be used by parents, caregivers, healthcare professionals, and educators to ensure that girls with autism receive the support and services they need to reach their full potential.

Personal stories and examples from girls with autism and their families to illustrate the experiences of those affected by autism.

Personal stories and examples from girls with autism and their families can provide valuable insight into the experiences of those affected by autism. These stories can help to raise awareness of the unique challenges faced by girls with autism and to illustrate the impact of these challenges on the lives of individuals and families. They can also provide hope and inspiration for others who are affected by autism, highlighting the strengths and resilience of those who have overcome diagnostic and other challenges.

One personal story that illustrates the experiences of a girl with autism and her family is that of a young girl named Mia. Mia was diagnosed with autism at the age of 4, after her parents noticed that she had difficulty with communication and socialization. Despite her diagnosis, her parents struggled to find appropriate support and resources for her. They found that most of the information and support they found was geared towards boys with autism, and they had a hard time finding programs and therapies that were tailored to Mia's specific needs.

Mia's parents found it challenging to understand and support her, as she had a hard time communicating her thoughts and feelings. She had a strong interest in music and art, but had a hard time participating in group activities. Her parents also found it hard for her to make friends, as she had difficulty understanding social cues and initiating conversations. Despite these challenges, Mia's parents were determined to give her the best life possible. They worked tirelessly to find the right resources and support to help her grow and develop.

As Mia grew older, her parents found that her interests and abilities changed. She became more interested in computer programming and coding. Her parents found a community college that offered a program for individuals with autism, which helped her to develop her skills and interests in technology. With the right support and resources, Mia was able to achieve her goals and has now landed a job in a tech company, where she is able to use her skills to improve the lives of others.

Another personal story is that of a young girl named Ava, who was diagnosed with autism at the age of 8. Ava's family noticed that she had difficulty with social interactions and communication, but they were not sure what was causing these difficulties. They took her to multiple doctors and specialists, but none of them could diagnose her with autism. It wasn't until Ava was 12 years old that she was finally diagnosed with autism, after her family found a doctor who specializes in diagnosing autism in girls.

This delay in diagnosis meant that Ava missed out on important early intervention services that could have helped her to develop the skills she needed to succeed in school and in social situations. Ava's family struggled to find appropriate support and resources for her, as most of the information and support they found was geared towards boys with autism. Despite these challenges, Ava's family was determined to give her the best life possible. They found a school that specialized in educating children with autism and provided her with the support she needed to succeed academically. They also found a therapist who specialized in helping individuals with autism develop social skills, which helped Ava to improve her ability to interact with others.

With the right support and resources, Ava was able to achieve her goals. She graduated from high school with honors and is now studying in college, where she is able to use her skills to help others.

In addition to these stories, there are many other examples of girls with autism and their families who have overcome diagnostic challenges and other obstacles. These examples can be found in books, articles, and online resources, and they can provide valuable insight into the experiences of those affected by autism. They can also serve as inspiration for others who are affected by autism, highlighting the strengths and resilience of those who have overcome diagnostic and other challenges.

These personal stories illustrate the experiences of girls with autism and their families, and how they faced diagnostic challenges, lack of resources and support, but with determination and the right resources they were able to overcome these challenges and achieve their goals. They also highlight the importance of early identification and intervention, specialized resources and support tailored to the unique experiences of girls with autism, and advocacy by families and caregivers in ensuring that girls with autism receive the support and services they need to reach their full potential.

Information on the unique symptoms and characteristics of autism in girls, as they may differ from those in boys.

Autism, also known as Autism Spectrum Disorder (ASD), is a neurodevelopmental disorder that affects an individual's ability to communicate, interact with others, and engage in repetitive behaviors. While autism is more commonly diagnosed in boys than in girls, recent research suggests that girls may present with unique symptoms and characteristics that differ from those in boys.

One key difference is that girls with autism may be better at hiding their symptoms and mimicking social cues. This is known as the "masking" phenomenon, and it can make it more difficult to diagnose autism in girls. Girls with autism may also be more likely to have a co-occurring condition, such as anxiety or depression, which can further mask their symptoms.

Girls with autism may be better at hiding their symptoms and mimicking social cues than boys with autism for a few reasons.

Firstly, girls are often expected to be more social and compliant than boys, which can lead to girls with autism working harder to hide their difficulties and conform to social expectations.

Secondly, girls with autism may be more motivated to fit in and be socially accepted. Therefore, they may be more likely to observe and mimic the social behaviors of their peers in order to blend in.

Thirdly, girls with autism may be better at understanding and interpreting social cues, such as tone of voice, facial expressions, and body language, which can help them to more effectively mimic the social behaviors of their peers.

Lastly, girls with autism may be less likely to exhibit some of the stereotypical behaviors associated with autism, such as repetitive movements or difficulty with eye contact, which can make it harder for healthcare providers to recognize the condition.

All these points can make it harder for healthcare providers to diagnose autism in girls, as the symptoms may not be as obvious and can be mistaken for other disorders. Therefore, specialized assessments, education and awareness for healthcare providers are crucial to ensure that girls with autism are accurately diagnosed and receive appropriate treatment and accommodations.

Another difference is that girls with autism may have a higher level of verbal ability compared to boys with autism. This means that they may be able to communicate more effectively and have a larger vocabulary, but they may still have difficulty with social communication and understanding nonverbal cues.

Girls with autism may have a higher level of verbal ability compared to boys with autism for a few reasons.

Firstly, girls tend to develop language skills earlier than boys and are more likely to have a larger vocabulary. This can make it easier for girls with autism to express themselves verbally and to understand and use language.

Secondly, girls with autism may be more motivated to use language to connect with others and may have more opportunities to practice their language skills in social settings.

Thirdly, girls with autism may be more adept at understanding and interpreting social cues, such as tone of voice and facial expressions, which can help them to better understand and use language in social situations.

It's important to note that these points are generalizations and may not apply to all individuals with autism, and some girls with autism may struggle with verbal communication. However, on average, girls with autism may have a higher level of verbal ability compared to boys with autism.

This can make it harder for healthcare providers to diagnose autism in girls, as it can be mistaken for other disorders such as language disorder. Therefore, specialized assessments, education and awareness for healthcare providers are crucial to ensure that girls with autism are accurately diagnosed and receive appropriate treatment and accommodations.

Girls with autism may also have a different set of interests and behaviors compared to boys with autism. For example, boys with autism may be more likely to engage in repetitive behaviors such as spinning or flapping, while girls with autism may be more likely to engage in solitary activities such as drawing or reading. Additionally, girls with autism may be more interested in social interactions than boys with autism, but may have difficulty initiating and maintaining social relationships.

Girls with autism may also have a different set of interests and behaviors compared to boys with autism. Some possible differences include:

Girls with autism may be more interested in social interactions and relationships than boys with autism. They may be more interested in talking to others, making friends and understanding social cues.

Girls with autism may also have different interests than boys with autism. They may be more interested in creative activities such as art or writing, or in helping others.

Girls with autism may also be more likely to have co-occurring mental health conditions such as anxiety or depression than boys with autism.

Girls with autism may have different coping mechanisms than boys with autism. They may be more likely to internalize their stress and emotions, and may be less likely to engage in self-stimulating behaviors.

Girls with autism may be less likely to be diagnosed with autism than boys with autism due to their ability to hide their symptoms and conform to societal expectations.

It's important to note that these points are generalizations and may not apply to all individuals with autism, and some girls with autism may have the same interests and behaviors as boys with autism.

However, on average, girls with autism may have a different set of interests and behaviors compared to boys with autism. This can make it harder for healthcare providers to diagnose autism in girls, as it can be mistaken for other disorders such as social anxiety or depression. Therefore, specialized assessments, education and awareness for healthcare providers are crucial to ensure that girls with autism are accurately diagnosed and receive appropriate treatment and accommodations.

It is important to note that autism is a spectrum disorder, and symptoms and characteristics can vary greatly from person to person. Therefore, it is important to evaluate each individual with autism on a case-by-case basis, rather than making assumptions based on gender.

In conclusion, there are unique symptoms and characteristics of autism in girls that may differ from those in boys. Girls with autism may be better at hiding their symptoms, have a higher level of verbal ability, and have different interests and behaviors compared to boys with autism. However, it is important to remember that autism is a spectrum disorder and that each individual should be evaluated on a case-by-case basis.

Examination of the social and cultural factors that may contribute to diagnostic challenges for girls with autism.

Autism Spectrum Disorder (ASD) is a neurodevelopmental disorder that affects an individual's ability to communicate, interact with others, and engage in repetitive behaviors. While autism is more commonly diagnosed in boys than in girls, research suggests that girls may present with unique symptoms and characteristics that differ from those in boys.

However, the diagnostic challenges for girls with autism are not limited to their symptoms alone, but also include social and cultural factors that may contribute to underdiagnosis and misdiagnosis.

One significant social factor that contributes to diagnostic challenges for girls with autism is the stereotype that autism is a "male disorder." This stereotype is based on the fact that autism is four to five times more common in boys than in girls. As a result, many healthcare professionals may be more likely to suspect autism in boys than in girls. This bias can lead to girls with autism being overlooked or misdiagnosed with other conditions, such as anxiety or depression.

Another social factor is the expectation that girls should be more socially adept and emotionally expressive than boys. Girls with autism may be better at hiding their symptoms and mimicking social cues, which is known as the "masking" phenomenon. This can make it more difficult to diagnose autism in girls, as they may appear to be more socially engaged and emotionally expressive than they actually are.

Social factors can also play a significant role in diagnostic challenges for girls with autism. Some possible social factors that may contribute to diagnostic challenges include:

Gender bias: Girls with autism may be less likely to be diagnosed than boys with autism due to gender bias in the diagnostic process. Research suggests that healthcare providers may be more likely to recognize and diagnose autism in boys, leading to underdiagnosis in girls.

Societal expectations: Girls with autism may face additional challenges in being diagnosed due to societal expectations of what it means to be a girl. For example, girls are often expected to be more socially adept, empathetic, and emotionally expressive than boys, which can make it harder to recognize the signs of autism in girls.

Limited understanding of autism in girls: There is still limited understanding and research on autism in girls, which can make it harder for healthcare providers to recognize and diagnose the condition in girls.

Stereotypical views of autism: Society often associates autism with males, and stereotypical views of autism can lead to girls with autism being overlooked or misdiagnosed.

Limited access to healthcare: Girls with autism from low-income families or from marginalized communities may face additional barriers to receiving a diagnosis and treatment due to limited access to healthcare.

<u>*Limited access to specialized assessments*</u>:
Girls with autism may face additional barriers to receiving a diagnosis and treatment due to lack of access to specialized assessments that take into account the unique presentation of autism in girls.

It's important to recognize and address these social factors in order to ensure that girls with autism receive accurate diagnosis and appropriate treatment and accommodations. This includes providing education and awareness for healthcare providers on the unique ways that autism can present in girls, and providing specialized assessments that take into account the unique presentation of autism in girls.

Additionally, providing support and resources for families and girls with autism, and promoting positive representation of girls with autism in media and society can help to reduce the negative stereotypes and misconceptions around autism that can make it harder for girls to get diagnosed and accepted in the society.

Culture also plays a role in diagnostic challenges for girls with autism. Different cultural groups may have different expectations and norms for social behavior and communication, which can affect how autism presents in girls. For example, in some cultures, it may be more acceptable for girls to be more reserved and independent, which can mask symptoms of autism. Additionally, some cultural groups may have limited access to healthcare resources, which can make it more difficult for girls with autism to receive a diagnosis.

Cultural factors can play a significant role in diagnostic challenges for girls with autism. Some possible cultural factors that may contribute to diagnostic challenges include:

Stereotypes and societal expectations: In many cultures, girls are expected to be more social and compliant than boys, which can lead to girls with autism working harder to hide their difficulties and conform to social expectations. This can make it harder for healthcare providers to recognize the signs of autism in girls.

Lack of awareness and education about autism: In some cultures, there may be a lack of awareness and education about autism, which can make it difficult for healthcare providers to accurately diagnose and treat girls with autism.

Different cultural understandings of autism: Different cultures may have different understandings of autism, which can lead to diagnostic challenges. For example, in some cultures, the focus may be on the child's behavior rather than their social and communication difficulties.

Language barriers: Girls with autism who come from cultures where English is not the primary language may face additional barriers to diagnosis and treatment. This is because they may have difficulty communicating with healthcare providers and may not have access to translated resources and assessments.

Stigma and discrimination: In some cultures, there may be a strong stigma and discrimination against individuals with autism, which can lead to diagnostic challenges. This is because parents and caregivers may be reluctant to seek help for their child due to fear of discrimination.

Cultural variations in parenting and child-rearing practices: Different cultures may have different parenting and child-rearing practices that can affect how autism presents in girls. For example, in some cultures, girls are expected to be more independent and self-sufficient from an early age, which can mask the symptoms of autism.

It is important to take these cultural factors into account when assessing and diagnosing girls with autism and provide culturally responsive care and support. This includes involving community and family members in the assessment and treatment process and providing resources in different languages and taking cultural considerations into account when developing interventions and accommodations.

Moreover, the diagnostic criteria for autism are based on research that has primarily focused on boys and men, which means that the diagnostic tools may not be sensitive enough to capture the unique symptoms and characteristics of autism in girls. This can lead to girls with autism being misdiagnosed or not diagnosed at all.

In conclusion, there are several social and cultural factors that contribute to diagnostic challenges for girls with autism. These include stereotypes that autism is a "male disorder," expectations that girls should be more socially adept and emotionally expressive than boys, and cultural norms and expectations that can affect how autism presents in girls.

Additionally, the diagnostic criteria for autism are based on research that has primarily focused on boys, which can lead to girls with autism being misdiagnosed or not diagnosed at all. It is essential for healthcare professionals to be aware of these factors and to approach the diagnosis of autism in girls with a holistic, individualized approach.

Information on the latest research and developments in the field of autism and how they relate to girls and women.

Autism Spectrum Disorder (ASD) is a neurodevelopmental disorder that affects an individual's ability to communicate, interact with others, and engage in repetitive behaviors. While autism is more commonly diagnosed in boys than in girls, recent research has begun to focus on the unique needs and experiences of girls and women with autism. The latest research and developments in the field of autism can be broadly categorized into four areas: diagnosis, symptomatology, interventions, and advocacy.

DIAGNOSIS

One of the most significant challenges in the field of autism is accurately diagnosing girls and women with autism. Research has shown that girls with autism are more likely to be overlooked or misdiagnosed with other conditions, such as anxiety or depression. In response to this, new diagnostic tools have been developed to specifically assess the unique symptoms and characteristics of autism in girls and women.

These tools take into account the "masking" phenomenon, which refers to the ability of girls with autism to hide their symptoms and mimic social cues. Additionally, there is ongoing research to understand the neurobiological differences between girls and boys with autism, which may lead to more accurate diagnostic criteria for girls.

Diagnosis being the latest research on autism affects girls and women with autism in a few ways. First, it can help to increase the understanding and recognition of autism in girls and women, as research has traditionally focused on boys and men with autism.

This increased understanding can lead to improved diagnosis and support for girls and women with autism. Additionally, the latest research on autism may also help to dispel stereotypes and misconceptions about autism, which can further improve support and understanding for girls and women with autism.

SYMPTOMATOLOGY

Symptomatology, or the study of symptoms, is a relatively new area of research on autism that is focused on understanding the specific ways in which autism presents in girls and women. This research is important because autism is often thought of as a disorder that primarily affects boys, and as a result, girls and women with autism may be underdiagnosed or misdiagnosed.

Research on the symptomatology of autism in girls and women has begun to highlight the unique differences between girls and boys with autism. For example, girls with autism are more likely to have a higher level of verbal ability, which can make it more difficult to diagnose autism.

Additionally, girls with autism may have different interests and behaviors compared to boys with autism, such as a greater interest in social interactions. This research is helping to create a more nuanced understanding of autism in girls and women, and to develop interventions that are tailored to their specific needs.

The research suggests that girls and women with autism may have different symptoms or may present their symptoms differently than boys and men with autism. For example, girls and women with autism may be better able to mask their symptoms or may have more subtle symptoms, such as difficulties with social communication or sensory processing, rather than the more obvious symptoms often associated with autism, such as repetitive behaviors or difficulty with language.

This research is important for increasing awareness of the ways in which autism can present in girls and women and for improving diagnosis and treatment for this population. It is also important for increasing understanding of autism in girls and women and for helping to reduce the stigma and discrimination often faced by individuals on the autism spectrum.

INTERVENTIONS

Interventions, or specific strategies and techniques used to support individuals with autism, is a key area of research on autism that is particularly important for girls and women with autism. This research is focused on developing and evaluating interventions that are tailored to the specific needs of girls and women with autism, as well as understanding the factors that influence the effectiveness of these interventions.

Research has also begun to focus on developing interventions that are specific to girls and women with autism. For example, studies have shown that social skills training is more effective for girls with autism than for boys with autism.

Additionally, research has found that girls with autism benefit from interventions that focus on building self-esteem and self-advocacy skills. These interventions can help girls with autism to better cope with the challenges they face, such as social isolation, and to build resilience in the face of adversity.

One key finding of this research is that girls and women with autism may benefit from interventions that are specifically designed to address the social and communication challenges that they may experience. For example, interventions that focus on building social skills, such as teaching individuals how to initiate and maintain conversations, or on teaching individuals how to interpret social cues, such as body language and facial expressions, may be particularly effective for girls and women with autism.

Another important finding is that interventions for girls and women with autism should also take into account the unique experiences and perspectives of girls and women, as well as the cultural and societal factors that may influence their experiences of autism. For example, interventions that address the unique experiences of girls and women with autism such as bullying, discrimination, and harassment, and providing a supportive, inclusive and safe environment could be beneficial for them.

Overall, intervention research on autism is critical for improving the quality of life for girls and women with autism and for helping them to reach their full potential.

ADVOCACY

Advocacy, or efforts to promote awareness and understanding of autism and to improve the lives of individuals with autism, is a key area of research on autism that is particularly important for girls and women with autism. This research is focused on understanding the barriers that girls and women with autism face and on developing strategies to overcome these barriers.

The latest research and developments in the field of autism have also led to increased advocacy for girls and women with autism. This includes the work of organizations such as the Autistic Women and Nonbinary

Network (AWN), which works to raise awareness of the unique needs and experiences of girls and women with autism.

Additionally, research has begun to focus on understanding the lived experiences of girls and women with autism, which can help to inform policy and advocacy efforts.

One important finding from advocacy research on autism is that girls and women with autism may face a number of unique challenges and barriers, such as a lack of understanding and awareness of autism in girls and women, and a lack of appropriate services and support.

Additionally, research has shown that girls and women with autism may be at a higher risk for experiencing bullying, harassment and discrimination, and may also be more likely to be misdiagnosed or undiagnosed.

Advocacy research also highlights the need for girls and women with autism to have representation and a voice in the autism community, and to have their needs and perspectives taken into account in research, policy, and practice. This can be done by increasing the participation of girls and women with autism in research studies and by involving them in decision-making processes related to autism.

Overall, advocacy research on autism is critical for increasing awareness and understanding of the experiences of girls and women with autism, and for improving the quality of life for this population by addressing the barriers they face and advocating for their rights and needs.

In conclusion, the latest research and developments in the field of autism have begun to focus on the unique needs and experiences of girls and women with autism. This includes new diagnostic tools, research on the symptomatology of autism in girls and women, interventions tailored to the specific needs of girls and women with autism, and increased advocacy for girls and women with autism. These efforts are helping to create a more inclusive and equitable understanding of autism and to ensure that girls and women with autism receive the support and resources they need.

A comprehensive list of resources and organizations that provide support and information for girls and women with autism.

There are a number of resources and organizations that provide support and information for girls and women with autism. These include:

The Autism Women's Network (AWN) is a non-profit organization that aims to provide support and resources for women and girls on the autism spectrum. They believe that autism is often misunderstood and underdiagnosed in women and girls, and they strive to raise awareness and understanding of the unique challenges and strengths of these individuals.

The Autism Women's Network (AWN) is an organization that provides support, resources, and information for women and girls on the autism spectrum. They offer a variety of programs, including mentoring, networking, and educational opportunities. The organization also has a website that features articles, videos, and other resources for women and girls with autism.

AWN offers a variety of resources and support services, including online forums, peer support groups, webinars, and a mentorship program. They also work to advocate for the needs and rights of autistic women and girls, and provide education and training to healthcare professionals, educators, and other professionals who work with this population.

AWN's mission is to provide a safe and supportive community for Autistic women and girls, to provide education and resources, and to promote visibility and acceptance of Autistic people. They also want to create opportunities for Autistic people to connect and support one another, and to advocate for the rights and needs of Autistic people.

AWN is a membership-based organization, with memberships open to anyone who identifies as a woman or girl on the autism spectrum, as well as allies and supporters.

The Asperger/Autism Network (AANE) is a non-profit organization that provides support, education, and resources to individuals with Asperger Syndrome and other autism spectrum conditions (ASC), as well as their families, partners, and professionals.

The Asperger/Autism Network (AANE) is another organization that provides support and resources for individuals on the autism spectrum, including girls and women. They offer a variety of programs, including counseling, social skills groups, and workshops. The organization also has a website that features articles and resources for individuals with autism.

Some services that AANE provides include counseling, coaching, social groups, and educational workshops. They also have an Adult Services program which helps adults with ASC navigate the challenges of daily living, find and maintain employment, and form healthy relationships.

In addition to their direct services, AANE also provides information and resources about ASC through their website, including a blog, articles, and fact sheets. AANE's mission is to help individuals with ASC understand and accept their differences, build meaningful and satisfying lives, and participate fully in the community.

The Organization for Autism Research (OAR) is a national non-profit organization that conducts and disseminates scientifically valid research, primarily in the areas of diagnosis, education, and treatment of autism spectrum disorder (ASD). OAR's mission is to apply research to improve the lives of individuals with autism and their families. They have a section of their website dedicated to providing information and resources for girls and women with autism.

OAR focuses on four main areas of research: early intervention, education, adult outcomes, and community participation. They also provide a range of resources, such as fact sheets and guides, to help educate and inform families, educators, and individuals on the latest research and best practices related to autism.

One of their key programs is the Research Grant Program which provides funding to scientists and researchers to conduct and disseminate autism research. They also have an Education Grant Program which provides funding to schools, programs, and organizations that support individuals with autism.

In addition to research and resources, OAR also provides education and training opportunities for professionals and families, such as webinars, workshops, and conferences.

Overall OAR is an organization that is focused on producing research-based knowledge about autism and making it accessible to individuals with autism, families, educators and other professionals in order to improve the lives of individuals with autism.

The National Autistic Society (NAS) is a UK based organization that provides support, information, and resources for individuals with autism, including girls and women. They offer a variety of programs, including support groups, social skills groups, and educational workshops. They also have a website that features articles and resources for individuals with autism.

NAS offers a wide range of services, including helplines, local support groups, and residential care homes. They also provide education and training for schools and other organizations to help them better support individuals with autism.

The NAS also provides a range of information and resources on their website, such as guides and fact sheets, on a wide range of topics related to autism. This includes diagnosis, education, employment, and benefits, as well as information for parents and carers.

The organization also has a campaign section that focuses on the concerns of the autism community and works to influence government policy and public opinion on issues that affect people with autism, such as education, housing, and employment.

NAS's goal is to help improve the lives of individuals with autism and their families by providing support, information, and campaigning for changes in policy and society.

The Autism Society of America (ASA) is a national organization that provides support, resources, and information for individuals with autism, including girls and women. The ASA was founded in 1965 and is the oldest and largest grassroots autism organization in the United States. They offer a variety of programs, including support groups, social skills groups, and educational workshops. The organization also has a website that features articles and resources for individuals with autism.

The organization's mission is to improve the lives of all affected by autism by increasing public awareness about the day-to-day issues faced by individuals with autism and their families, by advocating for appropriate services for individuals across the lifespan, and by providing the latest information regarding treatment, education, research and advocacy.

ASA provides a wide range of services and resources, including support groups, information and referral services, and a national conference. They also provide training and education to professionals and the general public to raise awareness and understanding of autism.

The organization also has a strong advocacy arm that works to influence public policy and legislation at the local, state, and national level to support the rights and needs of individuals with autism and their families. They also have a national network of affiliates across the US, which provide local support, services, and information to individuals and families affected by autism in their communities.

Overall, The Autism Society of America (ASA) is a national organization that provides support, education and advocacy to individuals with autism, their families, and the community.

The Autistic Self Advocacy Network (ASAN) is a US-based non-profit organization that is led and run by autistic individuals. ASAN's mission is to provide support and resources to the autism community, while working to empower individuals with autism to take control of their own lives and the direction of the autism rights movement. They have a website that features articles and resources for individuals with autism, as well as a number of programs and initiatives aimed at promoting the rights and inclusion of individuals with autism.

ASAN provides a wide range of services and resources to the autism community, including online resources, such as guides and fact sheets, and an online peer support community. They also provide training and education to individuals with autism, as well as to professionals and the general public, to raise awareness and understanding of autism.

The organization also has a strong advocacy arm that works to influence public policy and legislation at the local, state, and national level to support the rights and needs of individuals with autism and their families. They are particularly committed to ensuring that the voices and perspectives of autistic individuals are included in policy debates and decisions that affect them.

ASAN also provides opportunities for leadership development and community engagement for autistic individuals, including internships, volunteer opportunities, and leadership training programs.

Overall, The Autistic Self Advocacy Network (ASAN) is a national organization that is led and run by individuals with autism, which is focused on promoting self-advocacy and the rights and interests of individuals with autism through providing support and resources, community engagement, and influencing public policy.

Autistic Women & Nonbinary Network (AWN) is a US-based nonprofit organization that is led by and for autistic women and nonbinary people. Its mission is to provide support and resources for individuals who identify as autistic women and nonbinary people, while working to raise awareness and understanding of the unique experiences and perspectives of this community. They have a website that features articles, videos, and other resources for Autistic women, girls, and nonbinary people. They also have mentoring programs and online support groups.

AWN provides a variety of services and resources to the autism community, including online resources such as guides and fact sheets, and an online peer-support community. They also provide training and education to individuals who identify as autistic women and nonbinary, as well as to professionals and the general public, to raise awareness and understanding of the unique experiences and perspectives of this community.

The organization also has a strong advocacy arm, working to influence public policy and legislation at the local, state, and national level to support the rights and needs of autistic women and nonbinary people. They also advocate for the inclusion and representation of autistic women and nonbinary people in research, media, and policy discussions.

AWN also provides opportunities for leadership development and community engagement for autistic women and nonbinary people, including internships, volunteer opportunities, and leadership training programs.

Overall, Autistic Women & Nonbinary Network (AWN) is a US-based nonprofit organization that is led by and for autistic women and nonbinary people, with the mission of providing support and resources and raising awareness and understanding of the unique experiences and perspectives of this community.

These are just a few of the many organizations and resources available to girls and women with autism. It's important to note that autism is a spectrum disorder, and each individual with autism may have different needs and preferences when it comes to support and resources. Therefore, it's important to do research and explore different options in order to find the best fit for you or your loved one.

A guide on how to navigate the school and healthcare systems for girls with autism.

Navigating the school and healthcare systems can be challenging for any individual, but it can be especially difficult for girls with autism. There are a number of unique considerations and obstacles that parents and caregivers of girls with autism may face when trying to access the support and resources they need.

In terms of the school system, it is important to understand that girls with autism may experience a wide range of difficulties related to social interaction, communication, and behavior. They may also have difficulty with sensory processing, which can make it difficult for them to focus or stay engaged in a classroom setting.

To help girls with autism succeed in school, it is important to work with their school to develop an individualized education plan (IEP) that addresses their specific needs. This may include accommodations such as a quiet space for breaks, extra time on tests, or the use of assistive technology. It may also be helpful to work with a behavior therapist or social skills coach to help the girl develop the skills she needs to interact with her peers and succeed in the classroom.

Here are some guidelines for navigating school systems for girls with autism:

Understand the child's individual needs and strengths: Every child with autism is unique, so it's important to understand the child's specific needs and strengths.

Create a supportive learning environment: This includes providing a structured and predictable routine, using visual aids, and providing opportunities for social interaction.

Develop an individualized education plan (IEP): An IEP is a document that outlines the child's specific needs and the accommodations and services that will be provided to meet those needs.

Communicate with the school and other professionals: Regular communication with the school and other professionals, such as speech therapists and occupational therapists, can help ensure that the child's needs are being met.

Be an advocate for your child: It's important to be an advocate for your child and to ensure that their rights are being protected.

Be aware of gender specific aspects of autism: Girls with autism may present differently than boys, and this should be taken into account when providing support and services.

Encourage independence: Helping your child with autism to develop independence, self-care, and problem-solving skills can help them succeed in school and beyond.

Providing guidelines for navigating school systems for girls with autism is important for several reasons:

It helps ensure that the child's individual needs are met: Every child with autism is unique, and providing guidelines can help ensure that their specific needs are taken into account and addressed in a way that is tailored to them.

It helps create a supportive learning environment: Guidelines can help create a structured and predictable routine, use visual aids, and provide opportunities for social interaction, which can all help create a supportive learning environment for girls with autism.

It helps with the development of an individualized education plan (IEP): Guidelines can help ensure that an IEP is developed that addresses the child's specific needs and outlines the accommodations and services that will be provided to meet those needs.

It facilitates communication between school and other professionals: Guidelines can help ensure that regular communication occurs between the school and other professionals, such as speech therapists and occupational therapists, which can help ensure that the child's needs are being met.

It empowers parents/guardians to advocate for their child: Guidelines can provide parents/guardians with the information they need to advocate for their child's rights and ensure that their needs are being met.

It takes into account gender-specific aspects of autism: Guidelines specifically tailored to girls with autism can help ensure that their unique needs and strengths are taken into account and addressed.

It promotes independence in children: Guidelines can help children with autism develop independence, self-care, and problem-solving skills, which can help them succeed in school and beyond.

In terms of healthcare, it is important to remember that girls with autism may have different healthcare needs than neurotypical girls. For example, they may be more sensitive to certain medications or may have difficulty communicating their symptoms to a healthcare provider.

It is important to work with a healthcare provider who is familiar with autism and has experience working with girls on the spectrum. This may include a developmental pediatrician, a psychologist, or a psychiatrist. They can help to assess the girl's needs and develop a treatment plan that is tailored to her unique situation.

It may also be helpful to connect with local support groups for families of girls with autism. These groups can provide valuable resources, information, and support for parents and caregivers as they navigate the school and healthcare systems.

Here are some guidelines for navigating health systems for girls with autism:

Understand the child's individual needs and strengths: Every child with autism is unique, so it's important to understand the child's specific needs and strengths in regards to their health.

Find a healthcare provider who is experienced with autism: Look for healthcare providers who have experience working with individuals with autism and who understand the unique challenges that girls with autism may face.

Develop an individualized healthcare plan: Develop a plan that addresses the child's specific healthcare needs, including any related to autism.

Communicate with the healthcare provider and other professionals: Regular communication with the healthcare provider and other professionals, such as speech therapists and occupational therapists, can help ensure that the child's needs are being met.

Be aware of gender-specific aspects of autism: Girls with autism may present differently than boys, and this should be taken into account when providing support and services.

Be an advocate for your child: It's important to be an advocate for your child and to ensure that their rights are being protected.

Encourage independence: Helping your child with autism to develop independence, self-care, and problem-solving skills can help them succeed in navigating healthcare systems.

Educate yourself about the interventions and treatments that are available for autism, and be aware of the latest research and developments in this field.

Be aware of potential comorbid conditions that may accompany autism, such as gastrointestinal issues, sleep disorders and be prepared to address them accordingly.

Providing guidelines for navigating health systems for girls with autism is important for several reasons:

It helps ensure that the child's individual needs are met: Every child with autism is unique, and providing guidelines can help ensure that their specific needs are taken into account and addressed in a way that is tailored to them.

It helps find healthcare providers who are experienced with autism: Guidelines can help parents find healthcare providers who have experience working with individuals with autism, and who understand the unique challenges that girls with autism may face.

It helps develop an individualized healthcare plan Guidelines can help ensure that a healthcare plan is developed that addresses the child's specific healthcare needs, including any related to autism.

It facilitates communication between healthcare provider and other professionals: Guidelines can help ensure that regular communication occurs between the healthcare provider and other professionals, such as speech therapists and occupational therapists, which can help ensure that the child's needs are being met.

It empowers parents/guardians to advocate for their child: Guidelines can provide parents/guardians with the information they need to advocate for their child's rights and ensure that their healthcare needs are being met.

It takes into account gender-specific aspects of autism: Guidelines specifically tailored to girls with autism can help ensure that their unique needs and strengths are taken into account and addressed.

It promotes independence in children: Guidelines can help children with autism develop independence, self-care, and problem-solving skills, which can help them navigate healthcare systems.

It helps keep parents informed about the interventions and treatments that are available for autism, and the latest research and developments in this field.

It allows parents and healthcare provider to anticipate and address potential comorbid conditions that may accompany autism, such as gastrointestinal issues, sleep disorders, and other related issues.

In summary, navigating the school and healthcare systems for girls with autism can be challenging, but it is important to work with the right professionals and resources to ensure that the girl receives the support and accommodations she needs to succeed. Parents and caregivers should work closely with the school to develop an IEP, and healthcare providers who have experience working with girls on the spectrum. They can also connect with local support groups for families of girls with autism for additional resources and support.

A chapter on how to support girls with autism and their families in their daily life, including tips on communication, socialization, and independence.

Supporting girls with autism and their families in their daily lives can be a complex and nuanced task. Girls with autism may have unique challenges related to communication, socialization, and independence, and it is important to understand these challenges in order to provide the most effective support.

One of the most important aspects of supporting girls with autism is <u>communication</u>. Girls with autism may have difficulty communicating their needs, wants, and feelings, and it can be challenging for parents and caregivers to understand what they are trying to convey. To improve communication, it is important to use a variety of different strategies, including visual aids, social stories, and augmentative and alternative communication (AAC) devices.

Here are some tips for effective communication when assisting girls with autism and their families:

Use clear and simple language: Speak in a clear and simple manner, avoiding jargon or complex sentence structures, as this can be difficult for individuals with autism to understand.

Use visual aids: Visual aids such as pictures, diagrams, and videos can be helpful in communicating with girls with autism, as they may find it easier to understand information presented in this way.

Be patient: Girls with autism may take longer to process information, so be patient and give them time to respond.

Repeat important information: Repeat important information as needed, as girls with autism may have difficulty retaining information the first time it is presented.

Use nonverbal cues: Use nonverbal cues such as gestures and facial expressions to help convey meaning and build rapport with the child.

Encourage active listening: Encourage active listening by asking open-ended questions, repeating back what the child has said, and providing feedback.

Be respectful of the child's communication style: Every child is different and may have their own way of communicating, be respectful of their style and adapt to it.

Communicate with the parents/guardians: Regular communication with the parents/guardians can help ensure that the child's needs are being met and that everyone is on the same page.

Be aware of the child's developmental stage and adjust your communication accordingly: Girls with autism may be at different developmental stages, so it's important to adjust your communication style to meet their needs.

Be flexible: Be open to trying different communication methods and be willing to adjust them as needed to best support the child and their family.

Effective communication is essential in supporting girls with autism and their families in their daily lives. Here are a few ways in which communication can help:

Clear and consistent communication can help create a sense of predictability and structure in the child's environment, which can be beneficial for girls with autism.

Good communication can help ensure that the child's needs are being met, both in terms of their autism and any other related issues.

Communication can help build trust between the child, their parents/guardians, and professionals, which can make it easier for everyone to work together to support the child.

Communication can help identify and address any challenges or issues that may arise in the child's daily life, such as difficulty with self-care or social interaction.

Communication can help educate parents and professionals about the child's strengths and needs, which can help tailor the support provided to the child.

Communication can help promote independence in the child by providing them with the tools they need to express themselves and communicate their needs effectively.

Communication can be used as a tool to help the child understand and regulate their emotions.

Regular communication with teachers, therapists, and healthcare providers can ensure that the child's needs are being met in all areas of their life, and that interventions and treatments are working effectively.

Communication can help the child and their family to access support and resources, such as therapy, special education, and community services.

Open communication with the child and their family can help professionals understand the child's perspective and the impact of the disorder on their life, which can lead to more effective support.

<u>Socialization</u> is another key area where girls with autism may need support. Girls with autism may have difficulty interacting with their peers and may struggle to understand social cues and conventions. To help girls with autism develop social skills, it is important to provide opportunities for them to practice these skills in a safe and supportive environment. This may include social skills groups, playdates with other children, or social skills classes.

Here are some tips for effective socialization when assisting girls with autism and their families:

<u>Start with small steps</u>: Gradually introduce social interactions, starting with small and simple interactions and gradually building up to more complex interactions.

<u>Use visual aids</u>: Visual aids such as social stories, social scripts and social skills videos can be helpful in teaching girls with autism about social interactions and appropriate behaviors.

<u>Use role-playing</u>: Role-playing can be a helpful tool for teaching girls with autism about different social interactions and how to respond appropriately.

<u>Provide structured opportunities for social interaction</u>: Structured activities such as group games, sports, or clubs can provide opportunities for girls with autism to practice social interaction in a controlled environment.

<u>Encourage positive social interactions</u>: Encourage positive social interactions by praising the child for appropriate behavior and providing positive feedback.

<u>Address any problem behaviors</u>: If a child is displaying problem behaviors, it's important to address them directly and provide clear and consistent consequences.

<u>Provide social skills training</u>: Specialized social skills training can be effective in teaching girls with autism about social interactions and appropriate behaviors.

<u>Provide support in real-life settings</u>: Provide support in real-life settings such as school, the community and the family, this way the child can generalize the skills learned in a therapeutic setting.

<u>Be aware of gender-specific aspects of autism</u>: Girls with autism may present differently than boys, and this should be

taken into account when providing socialization support and services.

Communicate with the parents/guardians: Regular communication with the parents/guardians can help ensure that the child's needs are being met and that everyone is on the same page.

Socialization can play a critical role in supporting girls with autism and their families in their daily lives. Here are a few ways in which socialization can help:

Socialization helps individuals with autism learn how to interact with others: This can include learning how to initiate and maintain conversations, understanding social cues, and developing appropriate social behaviors.

Socialization helps individuals with autism develop social connections: This can include building friendships, participating in group activities, and learning how to navigate social situations.

Socialization can help individuals with autism improve their communication skills: This can include learning how to express themselves effectively, understanding and interpreting verbal and nonverbal communication, and learning how to respond appropriately to social cues.

Socialization can help individuals with autism to develop emotional regulation skills: This can include learning how to understand and manage their emotions, and how to cope with stress and anxiety.

Socialization can help individuals with autism to develop self-awareness: This can include understanding their own strengths and limitations, and being able to communicate their needs effectively.

<u>Socialization can help individuals with autism learn problem-solving skills</u>: This can include learning how to negotiate, collaborate, and resolve conflicts.

<u>Socialization can help individuals with autism to develop a sense of self-worth</u>: This can include learning how to advocate for themselves, and how to be proud of their accomplishments.

<u>Socialization can help individuals with autism to develop independence</u>: This can include learning how to take care of themselves, manage their time, and make their own decisions.

<u>Socialization can help individuals with autism to develop a sense of belonging</u>: This can include being part of a community, having friends, and learning how to participate in social activities.

Socialization can help individuals with autism to develop a sense of purpose: This can include learning how to set goals, plan and achieve them.

Another important aspect of supporting girls with autism is helping them to achieve <u>independence</u>. Girls with autism may have difficulty with self-care tasks, such as dressing, grooming, and personal hygiene. To help girls with autism become more independent, it is important to provide them with clear and consistent instructions and to break down self-care tasks into small, manageable steps.

Here are some tips for effective independence when assisting girls with autism and their families:

Understand the individual needs of the girl with autism: Every person with autism is unique and has their own set of strengths and challenges. It is important to understand the specific needs of the girl you are working with in order to provide effective support.

Involve the family: The family plays a crucial role in the development and well-being of a child with autism. It is important to involve them in the planning and implementation of interventions.

Use visual supports: Many individuals with autism are visual learners, so using visual supports such as pictures, charts, and diagrams can be helpful in teaching new skills and reinforcing existing ones.

Provide structure and routine: Individuals with autism often thrive in environments that are predictable and structured. Establishing a routine can help them feel more secure and less anxious.

Use positive reinforcement: Positive reinforcement can be an effective way to encourage appropriate behavior. This can include verbal praise, social recognition, and tangible rewards.

Address sensory needs: Many individuals with autism have sensory processing difficulties. Be aware of these needs and make accommodations such as providing noise-canceling headphones or a quiet space to retreat to.

Encourage social interaction: Social interaction is important for all children, but it can be particularly challenging for children with autism. Encourage social interaction through playdates, social skills groups, and other activities that involve peers.

Be patient and flexible: Working with individuals with autism can be challenging, but it is important to be patient and flexible. Remember that progress may be slow, but with time and patience, you can help the girl reach her full potential.

Independence can play an important role in supporting girls with autism and their families in their daily life in several ways:

Empowerment: Teaching girls with autism the skills they need to be independent can empower them to take control of their own lives and make their own decisions. This can improve their self-esteem and confidence.

Reducing caregiver stress: When a girl with autism is able to do more things independently, it can reduce the stress and burden on the caregivers, such as parents, who may have been providing constant assistance.

Improving daily functioning: Independence skills such as self-care, dressing, and grooming, meal preparation, and managing money can improve the girls' daily functioning and quality of life.

Enhancing social interaction: Independence skills such as social skills, communication, and problem-solving can enhance the girls' social interaction with their peers, family, and community.

Preparing for adulthood: Preparing girls with autism for independence as they grow older is crucial for their future, as it sets them up for greater success in adulthood. Skills such as independent living, self-advocacy, and self-determination can be very important in this aspect.

In summary, independence helps in supporting girls with autism and their families by empowering the girls, reducing caregiver stress, improving daily functioning, enhancing social interaction and preparing for adulthood.

In addition to these specific strategies, it is also important to create a supportive and understanding environment for girls with autism and their families. This may include

Educational support: Many girls with autism may require additional support in their education, such as specialized instruction, one-on-one tutoring, or assistive technology.

Behavioral interventions: Applied Behavior Analysis (ABA) and other evidence-based behavioral interventions can be effective in addressing challenging behaviors and teaching new skills.

Occupational therapy: Occupational therapy can help girls with autism develop fine motor skills, coordination, and other skills needed for daily living activities.

Speech therapy: Speech therapy can help girls with autism improve their communication skills and address any speech or language delays.

Mental health support: Girls with autism may benefit from mental health support such as counseling, therapy, and medication management.

Community involvement: Encourage the families to involve their girls in the community by participating in extracurricular activities, clubs, and volunteering opportunities.

Assistive technology: Assistive technology can provide a wide range of support for girls with autism, such as communication devices, apps, and software that can help with organization and task completion.

Access to resources: Provide the families with information about resources and support services available in their community, such as respite care, parent support groups, and financial assistance.

Advocacy: Advocating for the girls and their families in school, community and government can help to ensure that they receive the services and accommodations they need to thrive.

It's important to note that each girl with autism is unique and will have different needs, so a combination of these supports may be the most effective. It's also important to work closely with the families to ensure that any support provided is tailored to their specific needs and preferences.

It's also important to understand that each girl with autism is unique, and their needs and abilities may change over time. It is important to be open and flexible in the way you support them, and to work closely with professionals such as speech therapists, occupational therapists, and behavioral therapists to develop a support plan that is tailored to the girl's individual needs and abilities.

In summary, supporting girls with autism and their families in their daily lives requires a multifaceted approach that addresses communication, socialization, and independence. By using a variety of strategies and resources, and by creating a supportive and understanding environment, parents and caregivers can help girls with autism to achieve their full potential and lead fulfilling lives.

Conclusion

In conclusion, the topic of Girls with Autism: Overcoming diagnostic challenges is a critical issue that requires ongoing attention and action. Despite some progress being made in recent years, girls with autism continue to be underdiagnosed and overlooked, often due to a lack of understanding of the ways in which autism presents differently in girls and a lack of awareness and recognition of the signs and symptoms of autism in girls.

To overcome these diagnostic challenges, it is essential to raise awareness and understanding of the unique challenges that girls with autism face. This can be accomplished by increasing research on autism in girls, training healthcare professionals and educators to recognize the signs and symptoms of autism in girls, and working to create more inclusive and understanding environments for girls with autism.

In addition, it is important to recognize that girls with autism are a diverse population and that their experiences and needs may vary widely. Therefore, it is crucial to take a holistic and individualized approach when assessing and diagnosing girls with autism, taking into account not only their behaviors and symptoms, but also their unique strengths, interests, and experiences.

Furthermore, it is important to recognize that the diagnostic process for autism is not only about getting a label, but also about getting access to appropriate support and services. Therefore, it is crucial to ensure that girls with autism receive appropriate diagnosis, support, and accommodations that will help them to thrive.

Moreover, it is important to note that the diagnostic process for autism has been traditionally based on observations of boys, as the majority of studies have been conducted with male participants, which leads to a bias on how autism is perceived and diagnosed. However, recent studies have been conducted to understand the unique characteristics of autism in girls, which has led to a better understanding of the condition in girls.

In summary, overcoming diagnostic challenges for girls with autism is a complex and ongoing process that requires a multifaceted approach. By raising awareness and understanding of the unique challenges that girls with autism face, increasing research on autism in girls, and taking a holistic and individualized approach to assessment and diagnosis, we can work to ensure that girls with autism receive the support and services they need to thrive.